Classic

MEXICAN

Classic

MEXICAN

Hot and spicy recipes from all over Mexico

E L I S A B E T H   L A M B E R T   O R T I Z

ULTIMATE
E D I T I O N S

INTRODUCTION

Many of the foods we take for granted in the West were unknown before Christopher Columbus reached the Americas in 1492. The list is impressive. We had no corn (maize), tomatoes or peppers (sweet, pungent and hot); no common beans like red kidney or pinto beans; no pumpkins nor any other winter squashes. Courgettes and *chayotes* (*chocho*) were equally unfamiliar, as were avocados and guavas, and we had never tasted chocolate or vanilla. Even turkeys were unknown. All these foods originated in Mexico, where agriculture is believed to have been practised as long ago as 7000 BC, about the same time, give or take a century or two, as the cultivation of food crops began in the Middle East. After the Conquest of Mexico by Hernando Cortés, the Spanish introduced wheat and domesticated animals, hitherto unknown in the Americas. Cattle yielded beef, milk, butter, cream and cheese. The domestic pig, being better to eat, soon ousted the local wild and wily boar; lambs, goats and the domestic hen made their appearance. The Spanish planted olive trees for olive oil and walnut trees, as well as the vegetables that reminded them of home.

It was out of this meeting of Old and New Worlds that the cuisine of Mexico began to develop. This colonial kitchen still rests firmly on its Aztec and Mayan foundations and though it is unique in the world of cooking, it really is neither difficult nor inaccessible to recreate. Indeed, there are no difficult or complicated techniques to master and the unique flavours of Mexican dishes appeal to nearly everyone (and you don't have to love chilli in everything!).

Many famous and popular recipes make use of the

This page: The rich and varied terrains of Mexico provide a diverse harvest of produce, and next page (clockwise from top left): avocados, string of garlic, chayote, garlic bulb, tomatoes, onions, tomatillos, canned jalapeño chillies, courgettes, lemon and lime halves.

various types of unleavened flat pancakes made from corn (maize) flour which the Spanish called *tortillas*. This bread has the distinction of being made from cooked flour. Dried corn kernels are cooked in water with lime until soft, when the skins can be rubbed off. The corn is drained and ground to a heavy paste. The dried version is called *masa harina*, literally "dough flour". Although many Mexican women still make tortillas at home, some using the ancient skill of patting them out by hand, they can also be purchased uncooked or freshly-baked from *tortillerias*. Tortillas are also exported; you can now buy packets in most supermarkets. They are used as the basis of a number of dishes that the Spanish call *Antojitos*. More than just snack foods or starters, these little whims or fancies form a whole category in the Mexican kitchen.

Of equal importance in Mexican cooking is the family of cultivated capsicums that the Aztecs collectively called chilli, although we tend to differentiate between chillies and the mild-flavoured red, yellow and green peppers. It is estimated that there may be over a hundred varieties of chillies, some sold fresh, others pickled or dried. Chillies can irritate delicate skin and it is vital to wash your hands in warm soapy water immediately after handling them. Cooks with particularly sensitive skin should wear gloves.

The tomato is another ingredient essential to Mexican cooking, whether raw or cooked. There is another Mexican

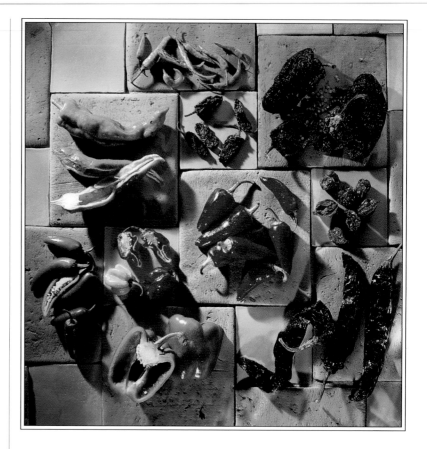

Clockwise from top left: small green chillies, chipotle chillies, mulato chillies, habanero chillies, pasilla chillies, green peppers, green jalapeño chillies, Anaheim chillies, and (centre left) Scotch bonnet chillies, (centre right) fresh red chillies.

tomato, the tomatillo (*Physalis ixocarpa*) which has an exquisite flavour. It is widely used in Mexico but is only as popular as the red tomato in Guatemala.

The Mexican kitchen is strongly regional. The cattle country of the north, bordering on Texas, is not good corn country and here the wheat flour tortilla is popular. It is always eaten with roast kid (baby goat), a northern favourite.

Much of the country is at altitudes of 7–8000 feet. Here the climate is temperate and all manner of fruits and vegetables flourish on the high plateau.

The semi-tropical regions at sea level have abundant tropical fruits and vegetables, including pawpaws (papayas), pineapples and coconuts. The extensive coastline yields a rich harvest of fish and shellfish. Before the Aztecs dominated the country, the Mayan Empire had flourished, invading Mexico's Yucatán peninsula and the southern part of the country. Here the cooking is subtly different. There are many regional chillies as well as unique herbs and spices. *Achiote* (annatto) is especially popular. The area boasts a sauce, *ixni-pec* (pronounced Schnee-peck), made with the *habanero* chilli – the hottest chilli in North America.

The ancient art of cooking in an earth oven still flourishes in Mexico. For *barbacoa* in the plateau, a pit is lined with the leaves of the agave plant. Heated stones are placed in the pit, the food (a whole lamb, vegetables and so on) is arranged on top and the pit is then sealed and the food left to cook. The agave gives a subtle flavour of tequila to the foods. In Yucatán, the earth oven is called a *pib*. It is lined with banana leaves and the meat, a suckling pig or maybe a chicken, is seasoned with achiote among other flavourings, and sprinkled with Seville orange juice, before being sealed in the pit and cooked.

In spite of industrialization, most people in Mexico prefer to eat their main meal, *comida*, in the middle of the day. This is a long, late lunch, often followed by a siesta. Soup is a must and so are beans. A small dish of beans (usually red kidney or pinto) are served separately after the main course and before dessert, which is often just fresh fruit. Breakfast is coffee with milk and a sweet bread. *Almuerzo*, a light meal which often bridges the gap between breakfast and *comida*, usually consists of a corn-based dish and although there may be a proper dinner, *cena*, served very late, more often the last meal is a light supper, *merienda*. This is often comprised of tamales and atole (corn gruel) with perhaps the addition of some sweet breads and jam.

RED ENCHILADAS

L iterally meaning "stuffed with chillies", *enchiladas* of all kinds are very popular snacks in Mexico.

INGREDIENTS
4 dried ancho chillies
450g/1lb tomatoes, peeled, seeded and chopped
1 onion, finely chopped
1 garlic clove, chopped
15ml/1 tbsp chopped fresh coriander
lard or corn oil, for frying
250ml/8fl oz/1 cup soured cream
4 chorizo sausages, skinned and chopped
18 freshly prepared unbaked Corn Tortillas
50g/2oz/2½ cups freshly grated Parmesan cheese
salt and freshly ground black pepper

SERVES 6

COOK'S TIP
Dipping the tortillas in sauce, then quickly cooking them in lard or oil, gives the best flavour. If you prefer, fry the plain tortillas very quickly, then dip them in the sauce, stuff and roll. There is not a great loss of flavour, and no spatter.

---

1 Roast the ancho chillies in a dry frying pan over moderate heat for 1–2 minutes, shaking the pan frequently. When cool, carefully slit the chillies, remove the stems and seeds, and tear the pods into pieces. Put in a bowl, add warm water just to cover, and soak for 20 minutes.

2 Tip the chillies, with a little of the soaking water, into a food processor. Add the tomatoes, onion, garlic and coriander; purée.

3 Heat 15ml/1 tbsp lard or corn oil in a frying pan. Add the purée and cook gently over a moderate heat, stirring for 3–4 minutes. Season to taste with salt and pepper and stir in the soured cream. Remove from the heat and set aside.

4 Heat a further 15ml/1 tbsp lard or oil in a small frying pan; sauté the chorizo for a few minutes until lightly browned. Moisten with a little sauce and set the pan aside.

5 Preheat the oven to 180°C/350°F/Gas 4. Heat 30ml/2 tbsp lard or oil in a frying pan. Dip a tortilla in the sauce. Add to the pan, cook for a few seconds, shaking the pan gently, turn over and repeat.

6 Slide the tortilla on to a plate, top with some sausage mixture, and roll up. Pack in a single layer in a baking dish. Pour the sauce over, sprinkle with Parmesan and bake for about 20 minutes.

CORN TORTILLAS

H ave ready a tortilla press and a small plastic bag, cut open and halved crossways.

INGREDIENTS
275g/10oz/2 cups masa harina
(tortilla flour)
250–350ml/8–12fl oz/
1–1½ cups water

MAKES ABOUT 14 × 14CM/
5½IN TORTILLAS

1 Put the *masa harina* into a bowl and stir in 250ml/8fl oz/1 cup of the water, mixing to a soft dough that just holds together. If it is too dry, add a little more water. Cover with a cloth and set aside for 15 minutes.

COOK'S TIP
Tortillas are easy to make but it is important to get the dough texture right. If it is too crumbly, add a little water; if it is too wet, add more *masa harina*. If you misjudge the pressure needed for flattening the ball of dough to a neat circle on the press, just scrape it off, re-roll it and try again.

---

2 Preheat the oven to 150°C/300°F/Gas 2. Open the tortilla press and line both sides with the prepared plastic sheets. Preheat a griddle until hot.

3 Knead the dough lightly and shape into 14 balls. Put a ball on the press and bring the top down firmly to flatten the dough out into a round.

4 Open the press. Peel off the top layer of plastic and lift the tortilla with the bottom plastic. Turn it on to your palm, so that the plastic is uppermost. Peel off the plastic and flip the tortilla on to the hot griddle.

5 Cook for about 1 minute or until the edges start to curl. Turn over and cook for a further minute. Wrap in foil and keep warm.

FLOUR TORTILLAS

ssential for stuffing, filling and wrapping all kinds of foods, tortillas are basic to Mexican food.

INGREDIENTS
225g/8oz/2 cups plain flour
5ml/1 tsp salt
15ml/1 tbsp lard or vegetable fat
120ml/4fl oz/½ cup water

MAKES ABOUT 14 × 15CM/ 6IN TORTILLAS

1 Sift the flour and salt into a mixing bowl. Rub in the lard or vegetable fat with your fingertips until the mixture resembles coarse breadcrumbs.

2 Gradually add the water and mix to a soft dough. Knead lightly, form into a ball, cover the bowl with a cloth and leave to rest for 15 minutes.

3 Divide the dough into about 14 portions and form into balls. Roll out each ball of dough in turn on a lightly floured board to a round measuring about 15cm/6in. Trim the rounds if necessary.

4 Heat a medium, ungreased griddle or heavy-based frying pan over a moderate heat. Cook the tortillas, one at a time, for about 1½–2 minutes on each side. Turn over with a large palette knife when the bottom becomes a delicate brown. Adjust the heat if the tortilla browns too quickly.

5 Stack the tortillas in a clean cloth if eating right away. Otherwise, wrap in foil and keep warm in the oven.

COOK'S TIP
Make flour tortillas whenever *masa harina* is hard to find. To keep them soft and pliable, make sure they are kept warm.

TACOS

T he taco has been called the Mexican sandwich; it is eaten in the hand, making a great, speedy snack. All you need is a supply of tortillas or taco shells, and a selection of fillings.

INGREDIENTS
freshly prepared Corn Tortillas
or pre-prepared taco shells

FOR THE FILLINGS
Picadillo, topped with guacamole
chopped chorizo, fried and mixed
with chopped Cheddar cheese
and chillies
Refried Beans (frijoles refritos),
with sliced jalapeño chillies,
Guacamole, and cubed cheese
leftover Mole Poblano de Guajolote
with guacamole
cooked shredded pork or chicken
with salsa and shredded lettuce

MAKE AS MANY AS YOU LIKE

COOK'S TIP
Filo pastry dries out very quickly and then becomes impossible to work with. Cover with a damp dish towel and take out one sheet at a time.

1 To make tacos, all you need is a supply of fresh corn tortillas, and as many of the suggested fillings as you can muster. The idea is to use your imagination, and cooks often vie with one another to see who can produce the most interesting combination of flavours. Chillies and guacamole are always welcome in the taco, or served as an extra on the side.

2 To make traditional soft tacos, simply spoon the filling on to the tortilla, wrap the tortilla around the filling, and eat.

3 To make hard tacos, secure the rolled up, filled tortilla with a cocktail stick, then briefly shallow fry until crisp and golden.

4 Pre-prepared U-shaped taco shells are not Mexican, but make a great speedy version of this snack. Hold one taco shell at a time in one hand, and fill with the fillings of your choice.

TORTILLA FLUTES

Flutes or *flautas* look as good as they taste and are particularly delicious accompanied by salsa, which can be found in most supermarkets.

INGREDIENTS
24 freshly prepared unbaked
Flour Tortillas
2 tomatoes, peeled, seeded and chopped
1 small onion, chopped
1 garlic clove, chopped
30–45ml/2–3 tbsp corn oil
2 freshly cooked chicken breasts,
skinned and shredded
salt
sliced radishes and stuffed green olives,
to garnish

MAKES ABOUT 12

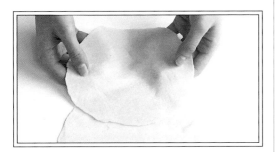

1 Place the unbaked tortillas in pairs on a work surface, with the right-hand tortilla overlapping its partner by about 5cm/2in.

2 Process the tomatoes, onion and garlic to a purée. Season with salt to taste. Heat 15ml/1 tbsp of the corn oil in a frying pan and cook the tomato purée for a few minutes, stirring to blend the flavours. Remove from the heat and stir in the shredded chicken, mixing well.

3 Spread about 30ml/2 tbsp of the chicken mixture on each pair of tortillas, roll them up into flutes and secure with a cocktail stick.

4 Heat a little oil in a frying pan large enough to hold the flutes comfortably. Cook more than one at a time if possible, but don't overcrowd the pan. Fry the flutes until light brown all over. Add more oil if needed.

5 Drain the cooked flutes on kitchen paper, and keep hot. When ready to serve, transfer to a platter and garnish with radishes and olives.

CORN SOUP

his is a simple-to-make yet very flavoursome soup. It can also be made with soured cream and cream cheese instead of the single cream.

INGREDIENTS
30ml/2 tbsp corn oil
1 onion, finely chopped
1 red pepper, seeded and chopped
450g/1lb sweetcorn kernels,
thawed if frozen
750ml/1¼ pints/3 cups chicken stock
250ml/8fl oz/1 cup single cream
salt and freshly ground black pepper
½ red pepper, seeded and cut in
small dice, to garnish

SERVES 4

1 Heat the corn oil in a frying pan and sauté the onion and red pepper until soft, for about 5 minutes. Add the sweetcorn and sauté for 2 minutes.

2 Carefully tip the contents of the pan into a food processor or blender. Process until smooth, scraping down the sides and adding a little of the stock, if necessary.

3 Put the mixture into a saucepan and stir in the stock. Season to taste with salt and pepper, bring to a simmer and cook for 5 minutes.

4 Gently stir in the cream. Serve the soup hot or chilled, sprinkled with the diced red pepper. If serving hot, reheat gently before adding the cream, but do not allow the soup to boil.

COOK'S TIP
Reheat the soup thoroughly and then add the cream off the heat. You don't have to stir the cream in completely: a few streaks and swirls look very pretty.

AVOCADO SOUP

vocado makes a delicious and creamy soup, which is beautifully complemented by the fresh coriander. Serve either hot or cold.

INGREDIENTS
2 large ripe avocados
1 litre/1¾ pints/4 cups chicken stock
250ml/8fl oz/1 cup single cream
salt and freshly ground white pepper
15ml/1 tbsp finely chopped coriander,
to garnish (optional)

SERVES 4

1 Cut the avocados in half, remove the stones and mash the flesh. Put it into a sieve and, with a wooden spoon, press it through into a warm soup bowl.

2 Heat the chicken stock with the cream in a saucepan over a gentle heat. When the mixture is hot, but not boiling, whisk it into the puréed avocado.

3 Season to taste with salt and white pepper. Serve immediately, sprinkled with the coriander, if using. The soup may be served chilled, if liked.

COOK'S TIP
The easiest way to mash avocados is to hold each stoned half in turn in the palm of one hand and mash the flesh in the shell with a fork, before scooping it into the bowl. This prevents the avocado from slithering about when it is being mashed.

TOMATO SOUP

 any cuisines offer a tomato soup, and Mexico's is deliciously fresh and simple.

INGREDIENTS
15ml/1 tbsp corn or peanut oil
1 onion, finely chopped
900g/2lb tomatoes, peeled, seeded and chopped
475ml/16fl oz/2 cups chicken stock
2 large fresh coriander sprigs
salt and freshly ground black pepper
coarsely ground black pepper, to serve

SERVES 4

1 Heat the oil in a large saucepan and gently fry the finely chopped onion, stirring frequently, for about 5 minutes, or until the onion becomes soft and transparent but not brown.

2 Add the chopped tomatoes, chicken stock and coriander sprigs to the pan. Bring to the boil, then lower the heat, cover the pan and leave the soup to simmer gently for about 15 minutes.

3 Remove and discard the coriander sprigs. Press the soup through a sieve and return it to the clean saucepan. Season to taste and heat through. Serve sprinkled with coarsely ground black pepper.

MEXICAN-STYLE RICE

Rice, apart from tortillas, is the most popular accompaniment for Mexican food.

INGREDIENTS
350g/12oz/1¾ cups long grain white rice
1 onion, chopped
2 garlic cloves, chopped
450g/1lb tomatoes, peeled, seeded and
coarsely chopped
60ml/4 tbsp corn or peanut oil
900ml/1½ pints/3¾ cups chicken stock
175g/6oz/1 cup cooked green peas
salt and freshly ground black pepper
4–6 small red chillies and
fresh coriander sprigs, to garnish

SERVES 6

1 Soak the rice in a bowl of hot water for 15 minutes. Drain, rinse well under cold running water, drain again and set aside.

2 Combine the onion, garlic and tomatoes in a food processor and process .

3 Heat the oil in a large frying pan. Add the drained rice and sauté until it is golden brown. Using a slotted spoon, transfer the rice to a saucepan.

4 Reheat the oil remaining in the pan and cook the tomato purée for 2–3 minutes. Tip it into the saucepan and pour in the stock. Season to taste. Bring to the boil, reduce the heat to the lowest possible, cover the pan and cook for 15–20 minutes until almost all the liquid has been absorbed.

5 Stir the peas into the rice mixture and cook, without a lid, until all the liquid has been absorbed and the rice is tender. Stir the mixture from time to time.

6 Transfer the rice to a serving dish and garnish with the drained chilli flowers (see Cook's Tip) and sprigs of coriander. Warn the diners that these elaborate chilli flowers are hot and should be approached with caution.

COOK'S TIP
Slice the red chillies from tip to stem end into four or five sections. Place in a bowl of iced water until they curl back to form flowers, then drain.

REFRIED BEANS

There is much disagreement about the translation of the term *refrito*. It means, literally, "twice fried". Some cooks say this implies that the beans must be really well fried, others that it means twice cooked. However named, *Frijoles Refritos* are delicious.

INGREDIENTS
90–120ml/6–8 tbsp lard or corn oil
1 onion, finely chopped
1 quantity Frijoles
(cooked beans)

TO GARNISH
freshly grated Parmesan cheese or
crumbled cottage cheese
crisp fried corn tortillas,
cut into quarters

SERVES 6–8

COOK'S TIP
Lard is the traditional (and best-tasting) fat for the beans but many people prefer to use corn oil. Avoid using olive oil, which is too strongly flavoured and distinctive.

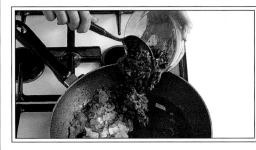

1 Heat 30ml/2 tbsp of the lard or oil in a large heavy-based frying pan and sauté the onion until it is soft. Add 225ml/8fl oz/ 1 cup of the *Frijoles* (cooked beans).

2 Mash the beans with the back of a wooden spoon or potato masher, adding more beans and melted lard or oil until all the ingredients are used up and the beans have formed a heavy paste. Use extra lard or oil if necessary.

3 Tip on to a warmed platter, piling the mixture up in a roll. Garnish with the cheese. Spike with the tortilla triangles, placing them at intervals along the length of the roll. Serve as a side dish.

CHAYOTE SALAD

C hayote goes by several different names – *chocho*, christophine or vegetable pear being the most familiar. Native to Mexico, they are now widely cultivated in the Caribbean, South East Asia and parts of Africa.

INGREDIENTS
2 chayotes, peeled and halved
1 large beefsteak tomato, about 225g/8oz,
peeled and cut into 6 wedges
1 small onion, finely chopped

FOR THE DRESSING
2.5ml/½ tsp Dijon mustard
30ml/2 tbsp mild white vinegar
90ml/6 tbsp olive or corn oil
salt and freshly ground black pepper
strips of seeded pickled jalapeño chillies,
to garnish

SERVES 4

COOK'S TIP
The seed of the chayote is edible and makes an admirable cook's perk.

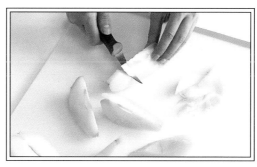

1 Leaving the seeds in place, cook the chayotes in a large saucepan of boiling salted water for about 20 minutes or until tender. Drain and leave to cool. Remove the seeds and set them aside (see Cook's Tip). Cut the flesh into chunks about the same size as the tomato wedges.

2 Make the dressing directly in a salad bowl. Combine the mustard and vinegar with salt and pepper to taste. Gradually whisk in the oil until well combined.

3 Put the chayote chunks, tomato wedges and finely chopped onion into a bowl. Add the dressing and toss gently together until well coated.

4 Put in a serving dish, garnish with the chilli strips and serve.

PEPPERS STUFFED WITH BEANS

Stuffed peppers are a popular Mexican dish. A special version – *Chiles en Nogada* – is served every year on August 28 to celebrate Independence Day. The green peppers are served with a sauce of fresh walnuts and a garnish of pomegranate seeds to represent the colours of the Mexican flag.

INGREDIENTS

6 large green peppers
1 quantity Refried Beans
2 eggs, separated
2.5ml/½ tsp salt
corn oil, for frying
plain flour, for dusting
120ml/4fl oz/½ cup whipping cream
115g/4oz/1 cup grated Cheddar cheese
fresh coriander sprigs, to garnish

SERVES 6

1 Roast the peppers over a gas flame or under a medium grill, turning occasionally, until the skins have blackened and blistered. Transfer the peppers to a plastic bag, secure the top and leave aside for 15 minutes.

2 Preheat the oven to 180°C/350°F/Gas 4. Remove the peppers from the bag. Hold each pepper in turn under cold running water and gently rub off the skins. Slit the peppers down one side and remove the seeds and ribs, taking care not to break the pepper shells. Stuff with the Refried Beans.

3 Beat the egg whites in a large bowl until they stand in firm peaks. In another bowl, beat the yolks lightly together with the salt. Fold the yolks gently into the whites.

4 Pour the corn oil into a large frying pan to a depth of about 2.5cm/1in and heat. Spread out the flour in a shallow bowl or on a flat plate.

5 Dip the filled peppers in the flour and then in the egg mixture. Fry in batches in the hot oil until golden brown all over. Arrange the peppers in an ovenproof dish. Pour over the cream and sprinkle with the cheese. Bake in the oven for 30 minutes or until the topping is golden brown and the peppers are heated through. Serve at once, garnished with fresh coriander.

GREEN LIMA BEANS IN SAUCE

A tasty and wholesome dish of lima beans, cooked in a tomato and chilli sauce.

INGREDIENTS
*450g/1lb green lima or broad beans,
thawed if frozen
30ml/2 tbsp olive oil
1 onion, finely chopped
2 garlic cloves, chopped
350g/12oz tomatoes, peeled,
seeded and chopped
1 or 2 drained canned jalapeño
chillies, seeded and chopped
salt
fresh coriander sprigs, to garnish*

SERVES 4

1 Cook the beans in a saucepan of boiling water for 15–20 minutes until tender. Drain and keep hot, to one side, in the covered saucepan.

2 Heat the olive oil in a frying pan and sauté the onion and garlic until the onion is soft but not brown. Add the tomatoes and cook until the mixture is rich and thick.

3 Add the jalapeños and cook for a further 1–2 minutes. Season with salt.

4 Pour the mixture over the reserved beans and check that they are hot. If not, return everything to the frying pan and cook over low heat for just long enough to heat through. Put into a warm serving dish, garnish with the coriander and serve.

CHOPPED COURGETTES

C *alabacitas* is an extremely easy recipe to make. If the cooking time seems unduly long, this is because the acid present in the tomatoes slows down the cooking of the courgettes.

INGREDIENTS

30ml/2 tbsp corn oil
450g/1lb young courgettes, sliced
1 onion, finely chopped
2 garlic cloves, chopped
450g/1lb tomatoes, peeled,
seeded and chopped
2 drained canned jalapeño chillies,
rinsed, seeded and chopped
15ml/1 tbsp chopped fresh coriander
salt
fresh coriander sprigs, to garnish

SERVES 4

1 Heat the oil in a flameproof casserole and add all the remaining ingredients, except the salt and coriander sprigs.

2 Bring to simmering point, cover and cook over a low heat for 30 minutes, or until the courgettes are tender. Check from time to time that the dish is not drying out, and if it is, add a little tomato juice, stock or water.

3 Season with salt and serve the Mexican way as a separate course. Alternatively, serve accompanied by any plainly cooked meat or poultry. Garnish with fresh coriander sprigs.

FRIJOLES

his basic method for cooking dried beans is the starting point for Refried Beans.

INGREDIENTS
350g/12oz/1¼–1½ cups dried red kidney, pinto or black haricot beans, picked over and rinsed
2 onions, finely chopped
2 garlic cloves, chopped
1 bay leaf
1 or more serrano chillies
(small fresh green chillies)
30ml/2 tbsp corn oil
2 tomatoes, peeled, seeded and chopped
salt
sprigs of fresh bay leaves, to garnish

SERVES 6–8

COOK'S TIP
In Yucatán, black haricot beans are cooked with the Mexican herb *epazote*.

---

1 Put the beans into a pan and add cold water to cover by 2.5cm/1in.

2 Add half the onion, half the garlic, the bay leaf and the chilli(es). Bring to the boil and cook vigorously for approximately 10 minutes. Put the beans and liquid into an earthenware pot or large saucepan, cover and cook over a low heat for 30 minutes. Add boiling water if the mixture starts to become dry.

3 When the beans begin to wrinkle, add 15ml/1 tbsp of the corn oil and cook for 30 minutes more, or until the beans are tender. Add salt to taste and cook for another 30 minutes, without adding more water.

4 Remove the beans from the heat. Heat the remaining oil in a small frying pan and sauté the remaining onion and garlic until the onion is soft. Add the tomatoes and cook for a few minutes more.

5 Spoon 45ml/3 tbsp of the beans out of the pot or pan and add them to the tomato mixture. Mash to a paste. Stir this into the beans to thicken the liquid. Cook for just long enough to heat through, if necessary. Serve the beans in small bowls and garnish with sprigs of fresh bay leaves.

AVOCADO AND TOMATO SALAD

A refreshing salad to accompany spicy dishes. To ripen avocados, put them in a brown paper bag and store in a dark place for several days, checking from time to time. They are ready when they yield to a gentle pressure at the stem end.

INGREDIENTS
2 ripe avocados
2 large beefsteak tomatoes, about
225g/8oz each, peeled and seeded
1 Iceberg lettuce, coarsely shredded, or
mixed salad leaves
30ml/2 tbsp chopped fresh coriander
salt and freshly ground black pepper

FOR THE DRESSING
90ml/6 tbsp olive or corn oil
30ml/2 tbsp fresh lemon juice

SERVES 4

1 Cut the avocados in half, remove the stones and peel off the skin. Cut the avocados and tomatoes into equal numbers of lengthways slices of approximately the same size.

2 Arrange a bed of shredded lettuce on a large platter and place the tomato slices on top. Arrange the avocado slices over the tomato and sprinkle with the coriander. Season to taste with salt and pepper.

3 To make the dressing, whisk the olive or corn oil and lemon juice together in a jug until well combined.

4 Pour a little dressing over the salad and serve the rest separately.

PRAWN SALAD

S alads in Mexico are usually served with the main course instead of green vegetables. Salads containing meat or seafood are served as a separate course, as they are very satisfying.

INGREDIENTS
1 Iceberg lettuce or 2 Little Gem
lettuces, separated into leaves,
or assorted lettuce leaves
60ml/4 tbsp mayonnaise
60ml/4 tbsp soured cream
350g/12oz cooked prawns,
thawed if frozen, chopped
75g/3oz/½ cup cooked
green beans, chopped
75g/3oz/½ cup cooked carrots, chopped
½ cucumber, about 115g/4oz, chopped
2 hard-boiled eggs, coarsely chopped
1 drained pickled jalapeño chilli,
seeded and chopped
salt

SERVES 4

COOK'S TIP
Use a crisp-leaved type of lettuce for a delightful contrast of texture with the other ingredients.

1 Line a large salad bowl or platter with the lettuce leaves. Mix the mayonnaise and soured cream together in a small bowl and put aside.

2 Combine the prawns, beans, carrots, cucumber, eggs and chilli in a separate bowl. Season with salt.

3 Add the mayonnaise and soured cream mixture to the prawns, folding it in very gently so that all the ingredients are well mixed and coated with the dressing. Pile the mixture into the lined salad bowl or arrange attractively on the platter and serve.

RED SNAPPER, VERACRUZ-STYLE

This is Mexico's best-known fish dish. In Veracruz, red snapper is always used for this recipe but fillets of any firm-fleshed white fish can be substituted successfully.

INGREDIENTS
4 large red snapper fillets
30ml/2 tbsp freshly squeezed lime or lemon juice
120ml/4fl oz/½ cup olive oil
1 onion, finely chopped
2 garlic cloves, chopped
675g/1½ lb tomatoes, peeled and chopped
1 bay leaf, plus a few sprigs to garnish
1.5ml/¼ tsp dried oregano
30ml/2 tbsp large capers, plus extra to serve (optional)
16 stoned green olives, halved
2 drained canned jalapeño chillies, seeded and cut into strips
butter, for frying
3 slices firm white bread, cut into triangles
salt and freshly ground black pepper

SERVES 4

1 Arrange the fish fillets in a single layer in a shallow dish. Season with salt and pepper, drizzle with the lime or lemon juice and set aside.

2 Heat the oil in a large frying pan and sauté the onion and garlic until the onion is soft. Add the tomatoes and cook for about 10 minutes until the mixture is thick and flavoursome. Stir the mixture from time to time, to stop it from catching on the base of the pan.

COOK'S TIP
This dish can also be made with a whole fish, weighing about 1.5kg/3–3½lb. Bake together with the sauce, in a preheated oven at 160°C/325°F/Gas 3. Allow 10 minutes cooking time for every 2.5cm/1in thickness of the fish.

3 Stir in the bay leaf, oregano, capers, olives and chillies. Add the fish and cook over a very low heat for about 10 minutes or until tender.

4 While the fish is cooking, heat the butter in a small frying pan and sauté the bread triangles until they are golden brown on both sides.

5 Transfer the fish to a heated platter, pour over the sauce and surround with the fried bread. Garnish with bay leaves and serve with extra capers, if you like.

CRAB WITH GREEN RICE

This delicious shellfish dish is a complete meal, as it is served ideally with green rice, an interesting variation on other rice dishes.

INGREDIENTS
225g/8oz/1 cup long grain rice
60ml/4 tbsp olive oil
2 × 275g/10oz cans tomatillos
(Mexican green tomatoes)
1 onion, chopped
2 garlic cloves, chopped
30ml/2 tbsp chopped fresh coriander
about 350ml/12fl oz/1½ cups
chicken stock
450g/1lb crab meat, thawed
if frozen, broken into chunks
salt and freshly ground pepper
chopped fresh coriander, to garnish
lettuce leaves, to serve

SERVES 4

1 Soak the rice in hot water and cover for 15 minutes; drain thoroughly. Heat the oil in a frying pan and sauté the rice over a moderate heat, stirring until the rice is golden and the oil has been absorbed.

2 Drain the tomatillos, reserving the juice, and put them into a food processor. Add the onion, garlic and coriander, and process to a purée. Pour into a measuring jug and add the tomatillo juice. Pour in enough stock to make the quantity up to 475ml/16fl oz/2 cups. Season to taste.

COOK'S TIP
Mexican cooks always soak rice in water before cooking it. This seems to pay off, as their rice is always delicious, with every grain separate.

3 Place the rice, tomato mixture and crab meat in a shallow pan. Cover and cook over a very low heat for about 30 minutes or until the liquid has been absorbed and the rice is tender. Serve on lettuce leaves, garnished with chopped fresh coriander.

PRAWNS WITH PUMPKIN SEED SAUCE

round pumpkin seeds give the sauce for this prawn dish a delicious and unusual texture.

INGREDIENTS
175g/6oz/1 generous cup pepitas
(Mexican pumpkin seeds)
450g/1lb raw prawns, thawed if frozen,
peeled and deveined
1 onion, chopped
1 garlic clove, chopped
30ml/2 tbsp chopped fresh coriander
225g/8oz tomatoes, peeled and chopped
1 drained canned jalapeño chilli, rinsed,
seeded and chopped
1 red pepper, seeded and chopped
30ml/2 tbsp corn oil
salt
whole cooked prawns, lemon slices and
fresh coriander sprigs, to garnish
rice, to serve

SERVES 4

1 Grind the pumpkin seeds finely, shake through a sieve into a bowl and set to one side.

2 Cook the prawns in boiling salted water. As soon as they turn pink, remove with a slotted spoon and set them aside. Reserve the cooking water.

3 Purée the onion, garlic, coriander, tomatoes, chilli, red pepper and pumpkin seeds in a food processor. Heat the oil in a pan, stir and cook the mixture for 5 minutes. Season with salt. Add prawn water to thin the mixture to a sauce consistency. Heat gently and add the prawns. Garnish with coriander sprigs and serve with rice.

SEVICHE

his makes an excellent starter for a summer meal. With the addition of sliced avocado, it could also make a light lunch for four.

INGREDIENTS
450g/1lb mackerel fillets,
cut into 1cm/¹/₂ in pieces
350ml/12fl oz/1¹/₂ cups freshly
squeezed lime or lemon juice
225g/8oz tomatoes, chopped
1 small onion, very finely chopped
2 drained canned jalapeño chillies or
4 serrano chillies, rinsed and chopped
60ml/4 tbsp olive oil
2.5ml/¹/₂ tsp dried oregano
30ml/2 tbsp chopped fresh coriander
salt and freshly ground black pepper
lemon wedges and fresh coriander,
to garnish
stuffed green olives, to serve

SERVES 6

1 Put the fish into a glass dish and pour over the citrus juice, making sure that the fish is totally covered. Cover and chill for 6 hours, turning once, by which time the fish will be opaque, "cooked" by the juice.

2 When the fish is opaque, lift it out of the juice and set it aside, reserving the juice.

COOK'S TIP
For a more delicately flavoured Seviche, use a white fish such as sole.

3 Combine the tomatoes, onion, chillies, olive oil, oregano and coriander in a bowl. Add salt and pepper to taste, then pour in the reserved juice from the mackerel. Mix well and pour over the fish.

4 Cover the dish and return the Seviche to the fridge for about an hour to allow the flavours to blend. Seviche should not be served too cold. Allow it to stand at room temperature for 15 minutes before serving. Garnish with lemon wedges and coriander sprigs, and serve with stuffed green olives sprinkled with chopped coriander.

PRAWNS IN SAUCE

T his colourful dish is called *Camarones en Salsa* in Mexico – serve it with rice, if you like.

INGREDIENTS
60ml/4 tbsp olive or corn oil
1 red pepper, seeded and chopped
2 large spring onions (white and green parts), chopped
2 garlic cloves, chopped
450g/1lb tomatoes, peeled, seeded and chopped
60ml/4 tbsp chopped fresh coriander
a little chicken stock
450g/1lb raw or cooked prawns, thawed if frozen, peeled and deveined
salt and freshly ground black pepper
fresh coriander, to garnish

SERVES 4

1 Heat the oil in a flameproof casserole and sauté the pepper, spring onions and garlic until the pepper is soft. Add the tomatoes and simmer for about 10 minutes or until the mixture is thick.

2 Add the coriander and salt and pepper to taste. If the sauce is very thick, thin with chicken stock.

3 Add the prawns and cook for about 2–3 minutes, depending on the size, until they turn pink. Be very careful not to overcook the prawns as they will toughen very quickly. Serve at once, with rice if liked, and garnish with fresh coriander.

FISH IN PARSLEY SAUCE

A simple, quick-to-make, delicious fish dish. Try to use flat leaf or continental parsley, which has much more flavour than curly parsley.

INGREDIENTS
275g/10oz can tomatillos
(Mexican green tomatoes)
1 onion, finely chopped
2 garlic cloves, chopped
50g/2oz/1 cup flat leaf parsley,
finely chopped
60ml/4 tbsp olive oil
6 firm-fleshed white fish fillets
salt and freshly ground black pepper

TO GARNISH
drained canned serrano chillies,
seeded, rinsed and shredded
sliced black olives

SERVES 6

1 Drain the tomatillos, reserving the liquid. Mash them in a bowl with the onion, garlic and parsley. Season with salt and pepper and set aside.

2 Heat the oil in a large frying pan and sauté the fish fillets until they are golden on both sides. Using a fish slice, transfer the fillets to a warmed serving dish, cover and keep hot.

3 Heat the oil remaining in the pan and add the tomatillo mixture. Cook over a moderate heat, stirring from time to time, until the sauce is well blended and has the consistency of single cream. If it is too thick, add a little of the reserved tomatillo juice. Season to taste with salt and pepper.

4 Pour the sauce over the fish fillets, garnish with the serrano chillies and black olives and serve.

SALT COD IN MILD CHILLI SAUCE

The salt cod has a very distinctive flavour that is particularly set off by the spicy sauce.

INGREDIENTS
900g/2lb dried salt cod

FOR THE SAUCE
6 dried ancho chillies
1 onion, chopped
2.5ml/½ tsp dried oregano
2.5ml/½ tsp ground coriander
1 serrano chilli, seeded and chopped
45ml/3 tbsp corn oil
750ml/1¼ pints/3 cups
fish or chicken stock
1 fresh green chilli, sliced, to garnish

SERVES 6

1 Soak the cod in cold water for several hours, depending on how hard and salty it is. Change the water once or twice during soaking, to reduce the saltiness.

2 Drain the fish and transfer it to a saucepan. Pour in water to cover. Bring to a gentle simmer and cook for 15 minutes, until tender. Drain, reserving the stock. Remove any skin or bones from the fish and cut it into 4cm/1½in pieces.

3 Remove the stems and shake out the seeds from the ancho chillies. Tear the pods into pieces, put in a bowl of warm water and soak until they are soft.

4 Drain the soaked chillies and put them into a food processor with the onion, oregano, coriander and serrano chilli. Process to a purée.

5 Heat the oil in a frying pan and cook the purée, stirring, for about 5 minutes. Stir in the fish or chicken stock and simmer for 3–4 minutes.

6 Add the prepared cod and simmer for a few minutes longer to heat the fish through and blend the flavours. Serve garnished with the sliced green chilli.

MOLE POBLANO DE GUAJOLOTE

ice, frijoles, tortillas and guacamole traditionally accompany this delicious, festive dish.

INGREDIENTS

2.75–3.6kg/6–8lb turkey
1 onion and 1 garlic clove, chopped
90ml/6 tbsp lard or corn oil
fresh coriander and 30ml/2 tbsp
toasted sesame seeds, to garnish

FOR THE SAUCE

6 dried ancho chillies
4 each dried pasilla and mulato chillies
1 drained canned chipotle chilli,
seeded and chopped (optional)
2 onions and 2 garlic cloves, chopped
450g/1lb tomatoes, peeled and chopped
1 stale tortilla, torn into pieces
50g/2oz/¹⁄₃ cup seedless raisins
115g/4oz/1 cup ground almonds
45ml/3 tbsp sesame seeds, ground
2.5ml/¹⁄₂ tsp coriander seeds, ground
5ml/1 tsp ground cinnamon
2.5ml/¹⁄₂ tsp ground anise
1.5ml/¹⁄₄ tsp ground black peppercorns
60ml/4 tbsp lard or corn oil
40g/1¹⁄₂ oz unsweetened (bitter) chocolate
15ml/1 tbsp sugar
salt and freshly ground pepper

SERVES 6–8

1 Joint the turkey into serving pieces. Put them into a saucepan or flameproof casserole large enough to hold them in one layer comfortably. Add the onion and garlic and cold water to cover. Season with salt, bring to a gentle simmer, cover and cook for about 1 hour or until tender.

2 Meanwhile, put the ancho, pasilla and mulato chillies in a dry frying pan over gentle heat and roast them for a few minutes, shaking the pan frequently. Remove the stems and shake out the seeds. Tear the pods into pieces and put these into a small bowl. Add sufficient warm water to just cover and soak, turning from time to time, for 30 minutes, until soft.

3 Dry the turkey pieces with kitchen paper. Reserve the stock. Heat the lard or oil in a large frying pan and sauté the turkey until lightly browned all over. Set aside. Reserve the oil.

4 Tip the chillies, with the water in which they have been soaked, into a food processor. Add the chipotle chilli, if using, with the onions, garlic, tomatoes, tortilla, raisins, ground almonds and spices. Process to a purée. Do this in batches if necessary.

5 Add the lard or oil to the fat remaining in the frying pan. Heat the mixture, then add the chilli and spice paste. Cook, stirring, for 5 minutes.

6 Transfer the mixture to the pan or casserole in which the turkey was originally cooked. Stir in 475ml/16fl oz/ 2 cups of the turkey stock (make it up with water if necessary). Chop and add the chocolate, and season with salt and pepper. Cook over a low heat until the chocolate has melted. Stir in the sugar. Add the turkey and more stock if needed. Cover the pan and simmer very gently for 30 minutes. Garnish with coriander and sesame seeds and serve.

PICADILLO

Serve as a main dish with rice, or this versatile recipe can be used to stuff peppers or fill tacos.

INGREDIENTS
30ml/2 tbsp olive or corn oil
900g/2lb minced beef
1 onion, finely chopped
2 garlic cloves, chopped
2 eating apples
450g/1lb tomatoes, peeled,
seeded and chopped
2 or 3 drained pickled jalapeño
chillies, seeded and chopped
65g/2½oz/scant ½ cup raisins
1.5ml/¼ tsp ground cinnamon
1.5ml/¼ tsp ground cumin
salt and freshly ground black pepper

TO GARNISH
15g/½oz/1 tbsp butter
25g/1oz/¼ cup slivered almonds
tortilla chips, to serve

SERVES 6

1 Heat the oil in a large frying pan and add the beef, onion and garlic and fry, stirring from time to time, until the beef is brown and the onion is tender.

COOK'S TIP
Do keep stirring the minced beef while it's browning, to break up any lumps.

2 Peel, core and chop the apples. Add them to the pan with all the remaining ingredients, except the garnishes and tortilla chips. Cook, uncovered, for about 20–25 minutes, stirring occasionally.

3 Just before serving, melt the butter in a small frying pan and sauté the almonds until golden brown. Serve the Picadillo topped with the almonds and accompanied by the tortilla chips.

VEAL IN NUT SAUCE

round nuts and soured cream combine to make an unusual sauce for veal.

INGREDIENTS
1.5kg/3–3½lb boneless veal,
cut into 5cm/2in cubes
2 onions, finely chopped
1 garlic clove, crushed
2.5ml/½ tsp dried thyme
2.5ml/½ tsp dried oregano
350ml/12fl oz/1½ cups chicken stock
75g/3oz/¾ cup very finely ground
almonds, pecan nuts or peanuts
175g/6fl oz/¾ cup soured cream
fresh oregano sprigs, to garnish
rice, to serve

SERVES 6

COOK'S TIP
Choose domestically raised pink veal if you can. It has a better flavour and tends to be more moist than white veal.

1 Put the cubes of veal, finely chopped onions, crushed garlic, thyme, oregano and chicken stock into a large flameproof casserole. Bring to a gentle boil. Cover tightly and simmer slowly over a low heat for about 2 hours, until the veal is cooked and tender.

2 Put the ground nuts in a food processor. Pour in 120ml/4fl oz/ ½ cup of the veal liquid and process for a few seconds until smooth. Press through a sieve straight into the casserole.

3 Stir in the soured cream and heat through gently, without boiling. Garnish with oregano. Serve at once with rice.

MEAT BALLS

Mexican cooks use twice-ground beef and pork for these *albondigas*. If preferred, the meat balls can be simply poached in beef stock.

INGREDIENTS
225g/8oz lean minced beef
225g/8oz minced pork
50g/2oz/1 cup fresh white breadcrumbs
1 onion, finely chopped
2.5ml/½ tsp dried oregano
or ground cumin
1 egg, lightly beaten
milk (optional)
corn oil, for frying
salt and freshly ground black pepper
oregano leaves, to garnish

FOR THE SAUCE
beef stock
1 chipotle chilli, seeded and chopped
1 onion, finely chopped
2 garlic cloves, crushed
225g/8oz tomatoes, peeled, seeded and
finely chopped

SERVES 4

1 Put the mixed beef and pork through a mincer or process in a food processor, if it is not already finely minced. Tip it into a bowl and add the breadcrumbs, onion and oregano or cumin. Season with salt and pepper and stir in the egg.

2 Knead thoroughly with clean hands to make a smooth mixture, adding a little milk if necessary. Shape the mixture into 4cm/1½in balls.

3 Heat 1cm/½in oil in a frying pan and fry the balls for 5 minutes, turning occasionally, until browned.

4 Put the meat balls into a shallow pan or flameproof casserole and pour over beef stock to cover. Add the remaining sauce ingredients and bring to the boil. Simmer for about 30 minutes. Using a slotted spoon, transfer the meat balls to a serving dish. Press the sauce through a sieve, then spoon it over the meat balls. Serve at once, garnished with oregano leaves.

LAMB STEW

his stew is known as *estofado de carnero* in Mexico. It has an interesting mix of chillies – the mild, full-flavoured ancho, and the piquant jalapeño which gives extra "bite". The heat of the chillies is mellowed by the addition of ground cinnamon and cloves.

INGREDIENTS
3 dried ancho chillies
30ml/2 tbsp olive oil
1 jalapeño chilli, seeded and chopped
1 onion, finely chopped
2 garlic cloves, chopped
450g/1lb tomatoes, peeled and chopped
50g/2oz/¹⁄₃ cup seedless raisins
1.5ml/¹⁄₄ tsp ground cinnamon
1.5ml/¹⁄₄ tsp ground cloves
900g/2lb boneless lamb,
cut into 5cm/2in cubes
250ml/8fl oz/1 cup lamb stock or water
salt and freshly ground black pepper
a few sprigs of fresh coriander, to garnish
rice, with herbs, to serve

SERVES 4

1 Roast the ancho chillies lightly in a dry frying pan over gentle heat to bring out the flavour.

2 Remove the stems, shake out the seeds, tear the pods into pieces and put them in a bowl. Pour in enough warm water just to cover. Leave to soak for 30 minutes.

3 Heat the olive oil in a frying pan and sauté the jalapeño chilli together with the onion and garlic until the onion becomes soft and tender.

4 Add the chopped tomatoes to the pan and cook until the mixture is thick and well blended. Stir in the raisins, ground cinnamon and cloves, and season to taste with salt and ground black pepper. Transfer the mixture to a flameproof casserole.

5 Tip the ancho chillies and their soaking water into a food processor and process to a smooth purée. Add the chilli purée to the tomato mixture in the casserole.

6 Add the lamb cubes to the casserole, stir to mix and pour in enough of the lamb stock or water to just cover the meat.

7 Bring to a simmer, then cover the casserole and cook over a low heat for about 2 hours or until the lamb is tender. Garnish with fresh coriander and serve with rice mixed with herbs.

CHICKEN IN GREEN ALMOND SAUCE

The bright green sauce, with the elusive flavour of almonds, complements the chicken.

INGREDIENTS
*1.5kg/3–3½lb chicken,
cut into serving pieces
475ml/16fl oz/2 cups chicken stock
1 onion, chopped
1 garlic clove, chopped
115g/4oz/2 cups fresh coriander,
coarsely chopped
1 green pepper, seeded and chopped
1 jalapeño chilli, seeded and chopped
275g/10oz can tomatillos
(Mexican green tomatoes)
115g/4oz/1 cup ground almonds
30ml/2 tbsp corn oil
salt
fresh coriander, to garnish
rice, to serve*

SERVES 6

COOK'S TIP
If the sauce seems a little pale, add 2–3 outer leaves of dark green cos lettuce. Cut out the central veins, chop the leaves and add to the food processor with the other ingredients.

1 Put the chicken pieces into a flameproof casserole or shallow pan. Pour in the stock, bring to a simmer, cover and cook for about 45 minutes, until tender. Drain the stock into a measuring jug and set aside.

2 Put the onion, garlic, coriander, green pepper, chilli, tomatillos with their juice and the almonds in a food processor. Purée fairly coarsely.

3 Heat the oil in a frying pan, add the almond mixture and cook over a low heat, stirring with a wooden spoon, for 3–4 minutes. Scrape into the casserole or pan with the chicken.

4 Make the stock up to 475ml/16fl oz/ 2 cups with water, if necessary. Stir it into the casserole or pan. Mix gently and simmer just long enough to blend the flavours and heat the chicken pieces through. Add salt to taste. Serve at once, garnished with coriander and accompanied by rice.

RICE PUDDING

Rice pudding is popular the world over and is always different. This version – *arroz con leche* – is light and attractive and very easy to make.

INGREDIENTS
75g/3oz/¹/₂ cup raisins
90g/3¹/₂oz/¹/₂ cup short grain rice
2.5cm/1in strip of lime or lemon peel
250ml/8fl oz/1 cup water
475ml/16fl oz/2 cups milk
225g/8oz/1 cup granulated sugar
1.5ml/¹/₄ tsp salt
2.5cm/1in cinnamon stick
2 egg yolks, well beaten
15g/¹/₂oz/1 tbsp unsalted
butter, cubed
toasted flaked almonds, to decorate
segments of fresh peeled
oranges, to serve

SERVES 4

1 Put the raisins into a small bowl. Cover with warm water and set aside to soak. Put the short grain rice into a saucepan together with the lime or lemon peel and water. Bring slowly to the boil and then lower the heat. Cover the pan and simmer very gently for about 20 minutes or until all the water has been absorbed.

2 Remove the peel from the rice and discard it. Add the milk, sugar, salt and cinnamon and cook, stirring, over a very low heat until all the milk has been absorbed. Do not cover the pan.

3 Discard the cinnamon stick. Add the egg yolks and cubed butter, stirring constantly until the butter has melted and the pudding is rich and creamy. Drain the raisins well and stir them into the rice. Cook the pudding for a few minutes longer.

4 Tip the rice into a dish and cool. Serve with the orange segments, decorated with the almonds.

COOK'S TIP
It is essential to use short grain rice for this pudding, which is sometimes called "pudding rice".

PUMPKIN IN BROWN SUGAR

This is a delicious way to make use of the abundance of pumpkin which is available at Hallowe'en.

INGREDIENTS
900g/2lb pumpkin, cut into wedges
350g/12oz/2 cups soft dark brown sugar
about 120ml/4fl oz/¹⁄₂ cup water
natural yogurt and brown sugar,
to serve (optional)

SERVES 4

COOK'S TIP
The best pumpkin for this recipe is the classic orange-fleshed variety used to make Hallowe'en lanterns. Choose one which will fit neatly into your casserole when cut.

1 Scrape the seeds out of the pumpkin wedges. Pack the wedges firmly together in a heavy-based flameproof casserole.

2 Divide the sugar among the pumpkin pieces, packing it into the hollows which contained the seeds.

3 Pour the water carefully into the casserole to cover the bottom and prevent the pumpkin from burning. Take care not to dislodge the sugar when pouring in the water.

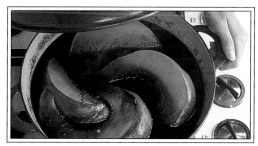

4 Cover and cook over a low heat, checking the water level frequently, until the pumpkin is tender and the sugar has dissolved in the liquid to form a sauce.

5 Using a slotted spoon, transfer the pumpkin to a serving dish. Pour the sugary liquid from the pan over the pumpkin and serve at once with natural yogurt, sweetened with a little brown sugar, if liked.

CHURROS

eep fried strips of batter are served drenched in sugar for this delicious hot dessert.

INGREDIENTS
250ml/8fl oz/1 cup water
15ml/1 tbsp granulated sugar,
plus extra for dusting
2.5ml/¹⁄₂ tsp salt
175g/6oz/1¹⁄₂ cups plain flour
1 large egg
oil, for frying
¹⁄₂ lime or lemon

MAKES ABOUT 24

COOK'S TIP
You can use a funnel to shape the *churros*. Close the end with a finger, add the batter, then release into the oil in small columns.

1 Bring the water, sugar and salt to the boil. Remove from the heat and beat in the flour until smooth.

2 Beat in the egg, using a wooden spoon, until the mixture is smooth and satiny. Set the batter aside.

3 Pour the oil into a deep frying pan to a depth of about 5cm/2in. Add the lime or lemon half, then heat the oil to 190°C/375°F/Gas 5 or until a cube of day-old bread added to the oil browns in 30–60 seconds.

4 Pour into a pastry bag fitted with a fluted nozzle. Pipe 7.5cm/3in strips of batter and then add to the oil, a few at a time. Fry for 3–4 minutes or until golden brown.

5 Using a slotted spoon, remove the *churros* from the pan and drain on kitchen paper. Roll the hot *churros* in granulated sugar before serving.

BUÑUELOS

his is one recipe out of many in Mexico which is based on a fried dough technique.

INGREDIENTS
225g/8oz/2 cups plain flour
5ml/1 tsp baking powder
2.5ml/¹⁄₂ tsp salt
15ml/1 tbsp granulated sugar
1 large egg, beaten
120ml/4fl oz/¹⁄₂ cup milk
25g/1oz/2 tbsp unsalted butter, melted
oil, for frying
sugar, for dusting

FOR THE SYRUP
225g/8oz/1¹⁄₃ cups soft light brown sugar
750ml/1¹⁄₄ pints/3 cups water
2.5cm/1in cinnamon stick
1 clove

SERVES 6

1 Make the syrup first. Combine all the ingredients in a saucepan. Heat, stirring, until the sugar has dissolved, then leave to simmer until the mixture has reduced to a light syrup. Remove and discard the spices. Keep the syrup warm while you then make the *buñuelos*.

2 Sift the flour, baking powder and salt into a bowl. Stir in the sugar. In a mixing bowl, whisk the egg and the milk well together. Gradually stir in the dry mixture, then beat in the melted butter to make a soft dough.

3 Turn the dough on to a lightly floured board and knead until it is smooth and elastic. Divide the dough into 18 even-size pieces. Shape into balls. With your hands, flatten the balls to disk shapes about 2cm/³⁄₄in thick.

COOK'S TIP
Make the syrup ahead of time if you prefer, and chill it until you are ready to use it, when it can be warmed through quickly.

4 Use the floured handle of a wooden spoon to poke a hole through the centre of each *buñuelo*. Pour oil into a deep frying pan to a depth of 5cm/2in. Alternatively, use a deep-fryer. Heat the oil to 190°C/375°F/Gas 5 or until a cube of day-old bread added to the oil browns in 30–60 seconds.

5 Fry the fritters in batches, taking care not to overcrowd the pan, until they are puffy and golden brown on both sides. Lift out with a slotted spoon and drain on kitchen paper. Dust the *buñuelos* with sugar and serve with the syrup.

COCONUT CUSTARD

This is another classic baked dessert. Alter the cinnamon and coconut to suit your tastes.

INGREDIENTS
225g/8oz/1 cup granulated sugar
250ml/8fl oz/1 cup water
7.5cm/3in cinnamon stick
115g/4oz/1 cup grated fresh coconut
750ml/1¼ pints/3 cups milk
4 eggs
175ml/6fl oz/¾ cup whipping cream
475ml/3 tbsp toasted chopped almonds (optional)

SERVES 6

1 Combine the sugar, water and cinnamon stick in a large saucepan. Bring to the boil, then lower the heat and simmer, uncovered, for 5 minutes. Remove the cinnamon stick.

2 Add the grated coconut to the pan, and cook over a low heat for 5 minutes more. Stir in the milk and cook, stirring from time to time, until the mixture has thickened to the consistency of thin custard. Remove from the heat and set aside.

3 Beat the eggs in a bowl until fluffy. Add a ladleful (about 45ml/3 tbsp) of the coconut mixture to the eggs and stir to mix. Continue to add the coconut mixture in this way, then return the contents of the bowl to the clean pan. Stir well.

4 Cook over a low heat, stirring constantly with a wooden spoon, until you have a thick custard. Pour into a serving dish.

5 Cool the custard, then chill until ready to serve. Whip the cream until thick and spread it over the custard. Decorate with toasted chopped almonds, if using.

COOK'S TIP
The easiest way to prepare a fresh coconut is to bake it in a preheated 180°C/350°F/Gas 4 oven for 15 minutes, then pierce two of the eyes with an icepick or sharp skewer and drain out the milk. Open the coconut by hitting it carefully with a hammer; it will break into several pieces, making it easy to remove the shell. Peel off the brown skin, chop the flesh into small pieces and grate in a food processor.

SANGRIA

T his very popular summer drink was borrowed from Spain. The Mexican version is slightly less alcoholic than the original.

INGREDIENTS
ice cubes
1 litre/1¾ pints/4 cups
dry red table wine
150ml/¼ pint/⅔ cup freshly
squeezed orange juice
50ml/2fl oz/¼ cup freshly
squeezed lime juice
115g/4oz/½ cup caster sugar
2 limes or 1 apple, sliced, to serve

SERVES 6

COOK'S TIP
Sugar does not dissolve readily in alcohol. Use simple syrup, which is very easy to make and gives a smoother drink. Combine 475ml/16floz/ 2 cups water and 450g/1lb granulated sugar in a jug and set aside until the sugar has dissolved. Stir from time to time. 15ml/1 tbsp simple syrup is equal to 7.5ml/1½ tsp sugar.

1 Half fill a large jug with ice cubes. Pour in the wine and the orange and lime juices.

2 Add the sugar (or syrup, see Cook's Tip) and stir well until it has dissolved. Pour into tumblers and float the lime or apple slices on top. Serve at once.

MARGARITA

T equila is made from the sap of a fleshy-leafed plant called the blue agave and gets its name from the town of Tequila, where it has been made for more than 200 years. The Margarita is the most popular and well-known drink made with tequila.

INGREDIENTS
½ lime or lemon
salt
120ml/4fl oz/½ cup white tequila
30ml/2 tbsp Triple Sec or Cointreau
30ml/2 tbsp freshly squeezed lime
or lemon juice
4 or more ice cubes

SERVES 2

COOK'S TIP
It really is worth going to the trouble of buying limes for this recipe. Lemons will do, but the special flavour of the drink will be lost in the substitution.

1 Rub the rims of two cocktail glasses with the lime or lemon. Pour some salt into a saucer and dip the glasses in so that the rims are frosted.

2 Combine the tequila, Triple Sec or Cointreau and lime or lemon juice in a jug and stir to mix well.

3 Pour the tequila mixture into the prepared glasses. Add the ice cubes and serve at once.

ROSELLA DRINK

n Mexico, the bright red sepals of a tropical flowering plant, *Hibiscus sabdariffa*, are used to make drinks. Available fresh in the Caribbean at Christmas and dried at other times, the plant is known in Mexico as *Flor de Jamaica* and elsewhere as *rosella* and *sorrel*. This drink is known as *Agua de Jamaica*.

INGREDIENTS
1 litre/1¾ pints/4 cups water
50g/2oz rosella sepals
a little granulated sugar

SERVES 4

2 Allow to boil gently, uncovered, for 1 minute, then remove from the heat and leave to stand for 15 minutes. Stir in a little sugar to sweeten. Strain into a jug. Cool, then cover and chill very well.

3 Serve the ice-cold Rosella Drink in long tumblers filled with ice.

1 Combine the water and *rosella* sepals in a large saucepan. Bring to the boil over a moderate heat.

COOK'S TIP
This soft drink can be made very festive with the addition of light rum. Mix 50ml/2fl oz light rum with an equal amount of Rosella Drink per serving.

CHOCOLATE CORN DRINK

I n Mexico, drinking chocolate is beaten with a very pretty carved wooden *molinillo*, but a wire whisk does the job just as well if not so decoratively. This traditional drink also contains *masa harina* and is known in Mexico as *champurrado*.

INGREDIENTS
50g/2oz/¹⁄₂ cup masa harina
(tortilla flour)
750ml/1¹⁄₄ pints/3 cups plain water
5cm/2in cinnamon stick
750ml/1¹⁄₄ pints/3 cups milk
75g/3oz/3 squares Mexican chocolate,
or any unsweetened (bitter)
chocolate, grated
a little soft light brown sugar

SERVES 6

COOK'S TIP
If Mexican chocolate isn't available, use unsweetened (bitter) chocolate instead.

1 Combine the *masa harina* and water in a large saucepan, stirring to mix well. Add the cinnamon stick and cook, stirring over a low heat, until the mixture has become thick.

2 Gradually stir in the milk, then the grated chocolate. Continue to cook until all the chocolate has dissolved, beating with a whisk or a Mexican *molinillo*. Discard the cinnamon stick. Sweeten to taste with brown sugar. Serve hot in cups.

ROMPOPE

This drink could best be described as cooked eggnog. It keeps well if chilled but seldom gets the chance – it's so delicious it tends to vanish as if by magic! Serve as an aperitif or liqueur.

INGREDIENTS
1 litre/1¾ pints/4 cups milk
225g/8oz/1 cup granulated sugar
5cm/2in cinnamon stick
50g/2oz/½ cup ground almonds
12 large egg yolks
475ml/16fl oz/2 cups medium rum

MAKES ABOUT 1.75 LITRES/
3 PINTS/7½ CUPS

COOK'S TIP
Try serving this over lots of ice in a tall tumbler for a deliciously long drink.

1 Combine the milk, sugar and cinnamon in a large saucepan. Simmer over a very low heat, stirring constantly, until the sugar has dissolved.

2 Cool to room temperature. Remove the cinnamon stick and then stir in the ground almonds.

3 Beat the egg yolks in a bowl until they are very thick and pale.

4 Add the egg yolks to the almond mixture a little at a time, beating well. Return the pan to the heat and cook gently until the mixture coats a spoon. Cool.

5 Stir in the rum. Pour into a clean dry bottle and cork tightly. Keep in the fridge for 2 days before serving.

INDEX